THE ADVENTURES OF WIN AND WIL

THE BIRTHDAY
CELEBRATION

Activity and Coloring Book
for ages 4-8

WRITTEN BY: MAISHA JACK
ILLUSTRATED BY: MARIA AKRAM

JANUARY

				1	2	3
4	5	6	7	8	9	10
11	12	13	14	15	16	(17)
18	19	20	21	22	23	24
25	26	27	28	29	30	31

Map of Massachusetts

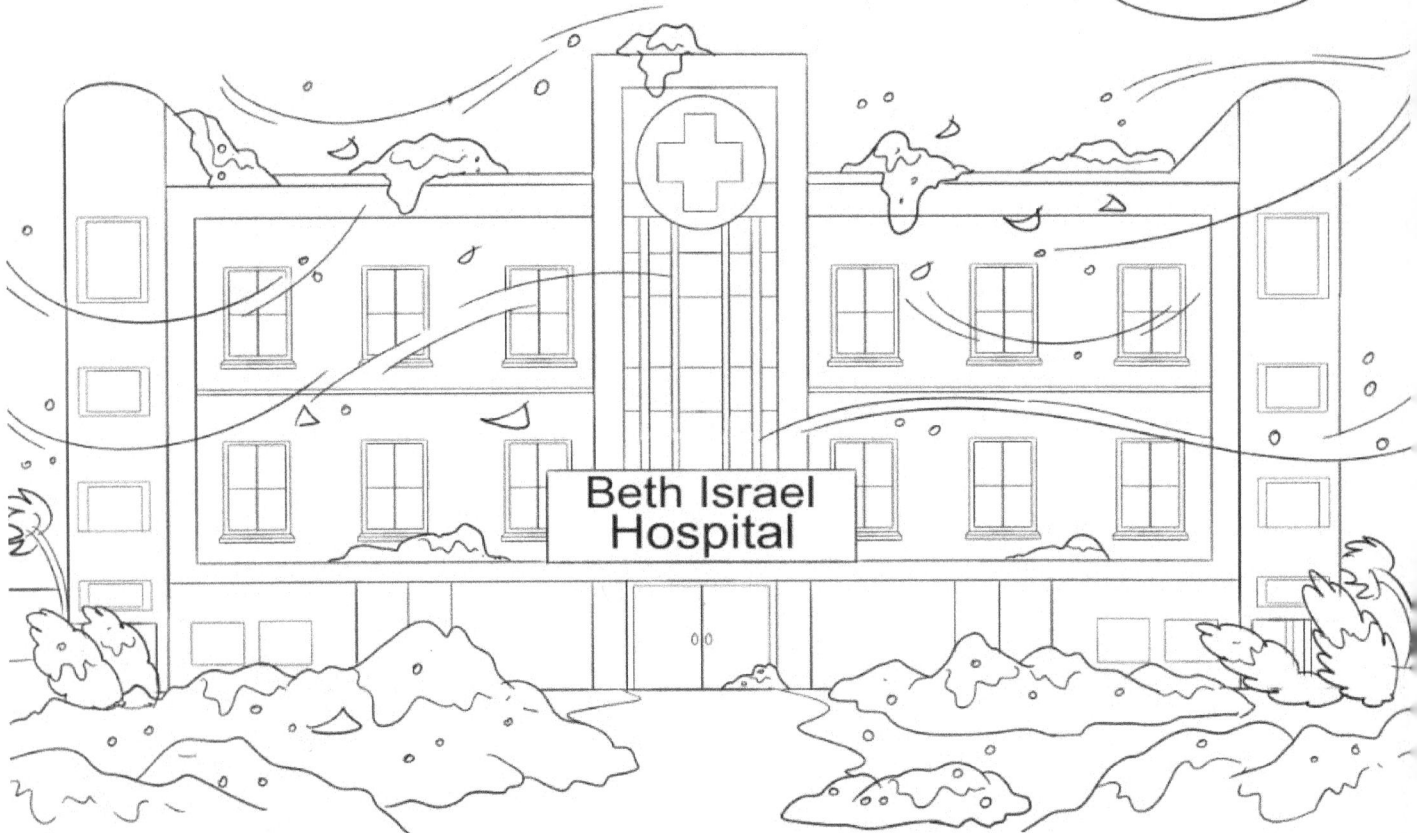

Boston

Dorchester

Beth Israel
Hospital

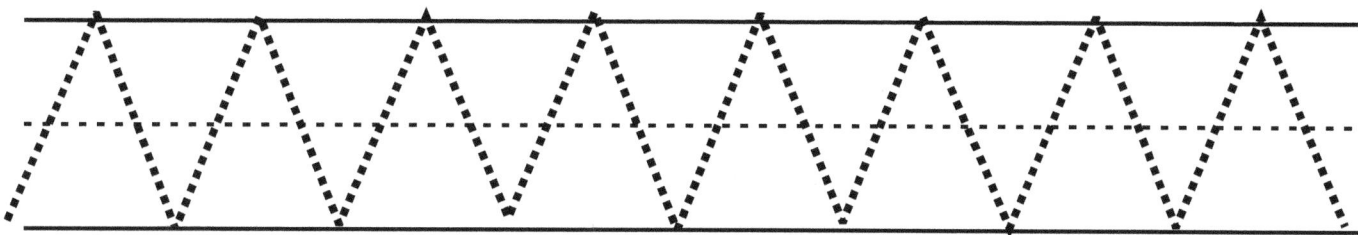

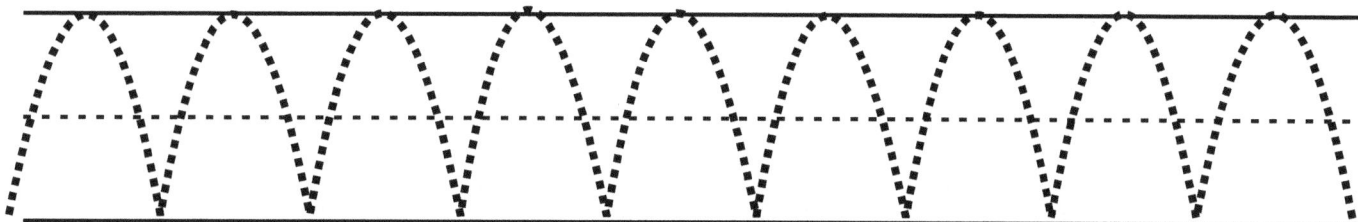

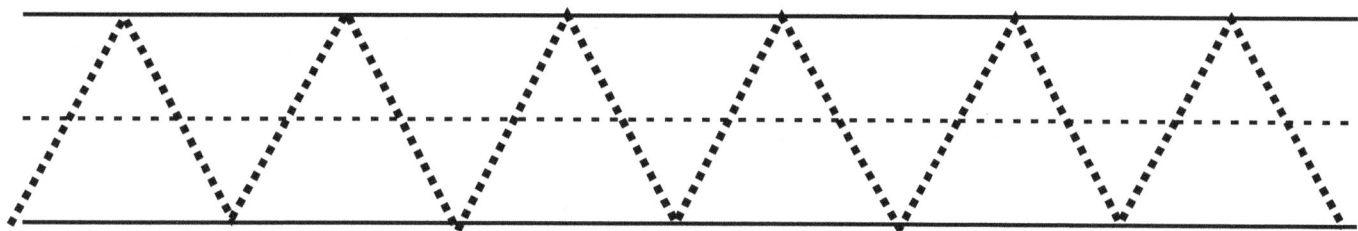

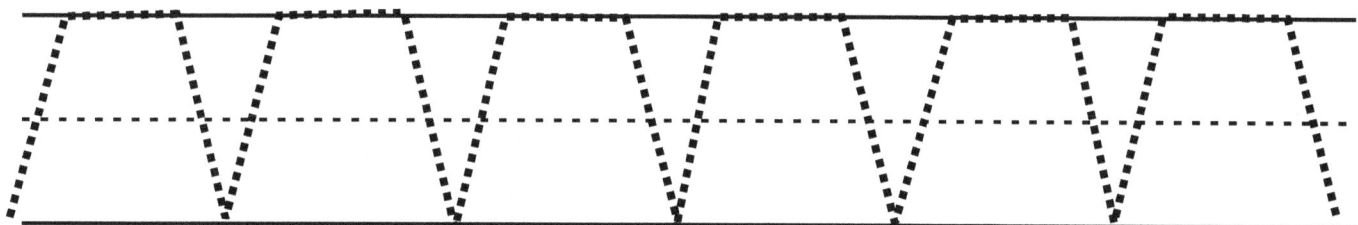

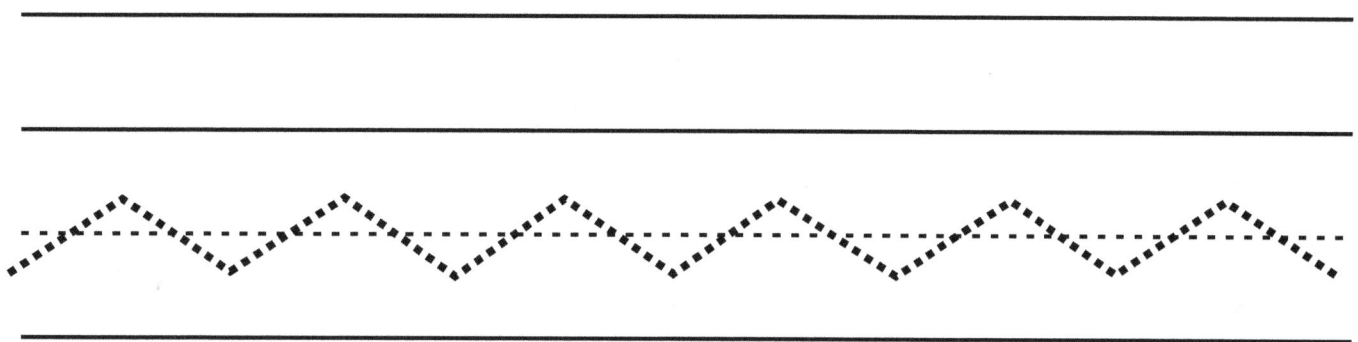

WORD SEARCH

```
G R A Y R U D U B X X U T E E
D C H N I N T E N D O X W S T
I J A N U A R Y G M U K I X R
N V P U P I L C A N D Y N W X
J Y P N F X G Z W D H I S I L
Z B Y R Z I R J J X T N C N C
L A W R E N C E M K S Y P S A
O A B I R T H D A Y F A Q T R
U G J D V I C E L T I C S O S
N X Q Z P S U P F W L B J N J
E P N T V E Y J A I Z P S I D
D C O O K I E S B L H B Z N R
T P A T R I O T S T I L W P U
C M L T W E T L G O D U J O P
N S Q K H T W V B N B E T A D
```

WINSTON	PATRIOTS	GRAY
WILTON	CARS	BLUE
LAWRENCE	CANDY	NINTENDO
COOKIES	TWINS	BIRTHDAY
CELTICS	HAPPY	JANUARY

CIRCLE THE CORRECT NUMBER

| 2 | 5 | 9 |

| 8 | 6 | 2 |

| 1 | 4 | 5 |

| 6 | 7 | 9 |

| 4 | 3 | 8 |

| 7 | 3 | 5 |

IN THE BOX, DRAW A PICTURE OF YOU PLAYING YOUR FAVORITE SPORT.

CONNECT DOT TO DOT AND COLOR

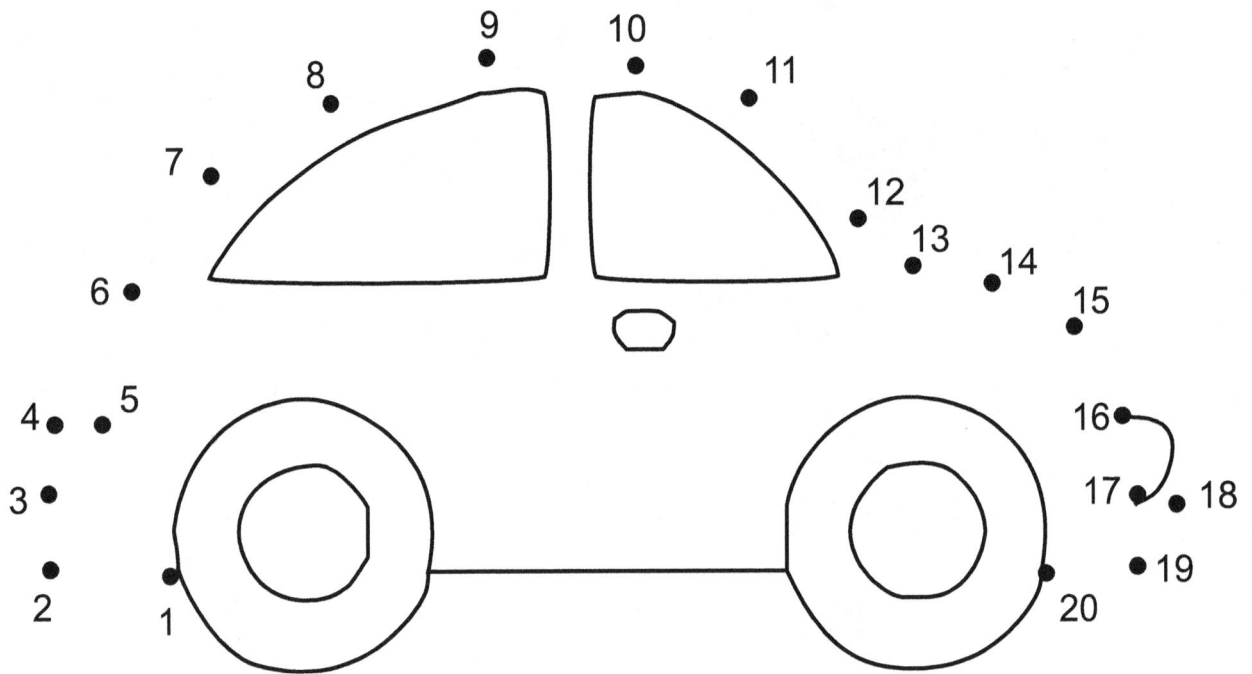

9
8
10
11
7
12
13
6
14
15
4 5
16
3
17 18
2 1
20
19

COUNT AND COLOR

3	
2	
1	
5	
4	

MATCH THE SHADOW

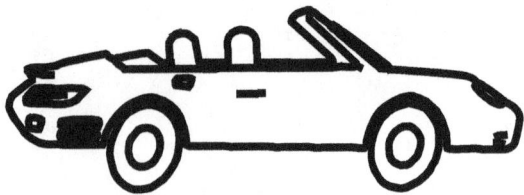

HAPPY BIRTHDAY

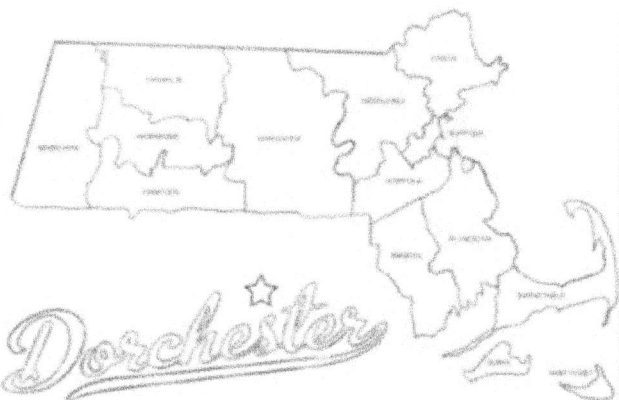

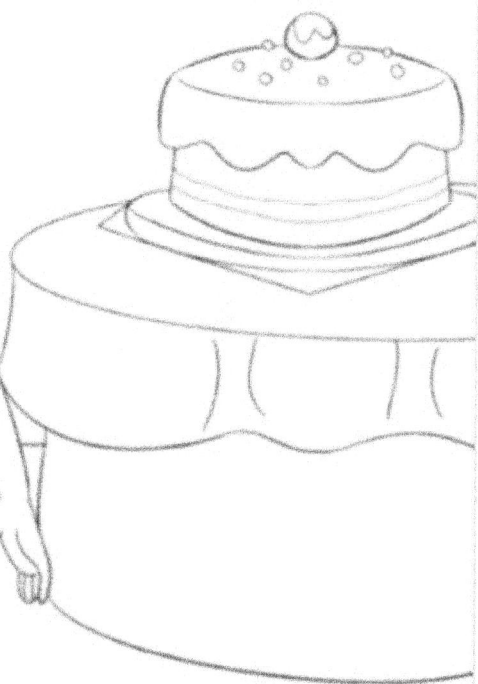

Dorchester

FILL THE PATTERN

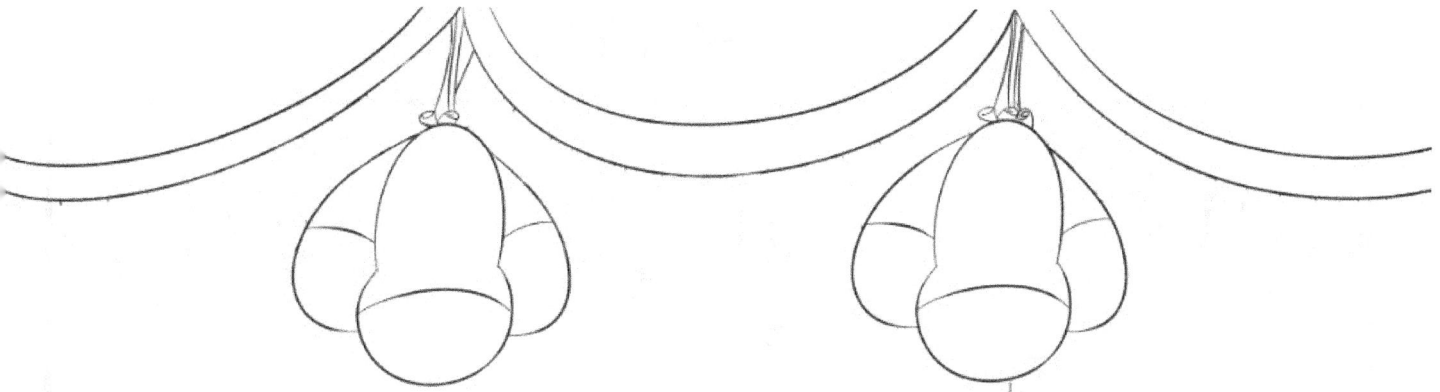

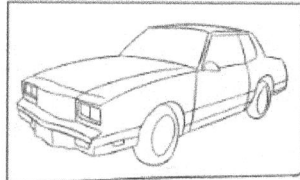

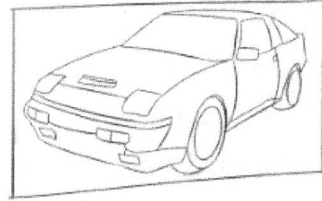

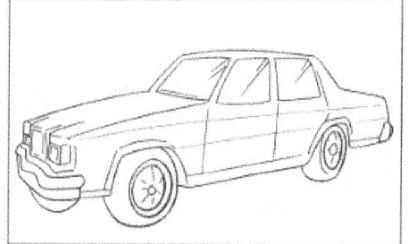

HOW MANY?

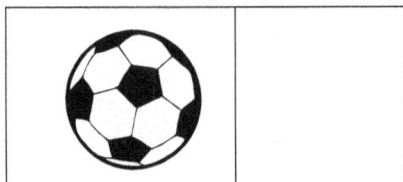

Joseph Estabrook
Elementary School

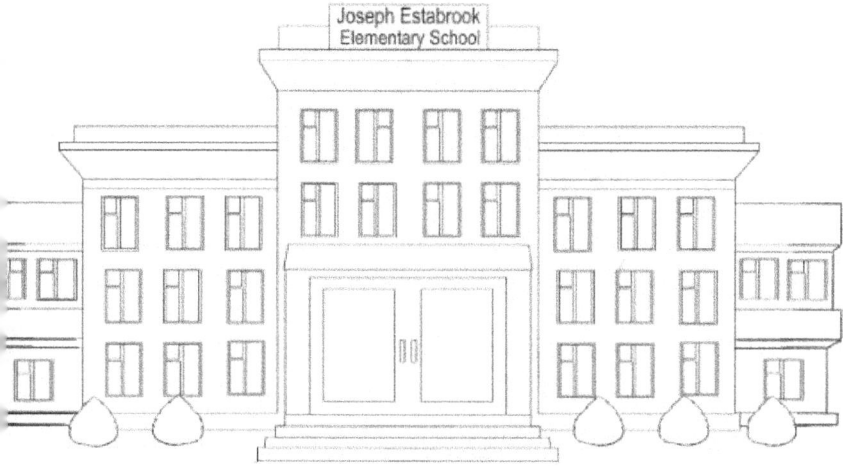

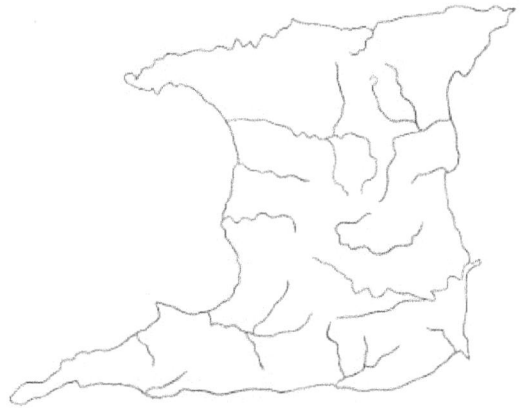

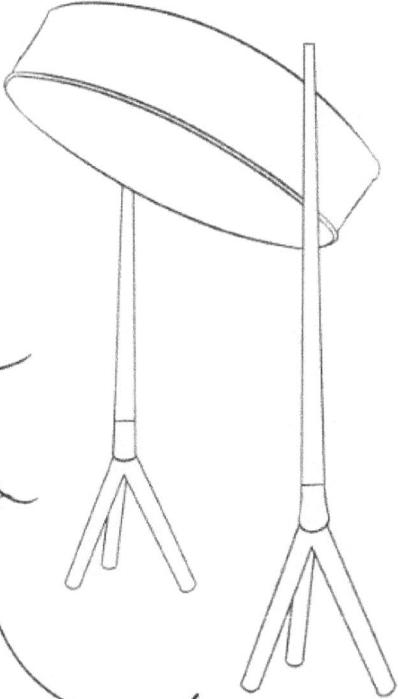

NEW ENGLAND PATRIOTS

BOSTON CELTICS

About the Author

Maisha Jack, Ed.S, an Amazon #1 Best Selling Author, was born and raised in Winchester, Kentucky, excelling in academics, basketball and track. Maisha has been an educator in Kentucky and in Georgia for the past 24 years, serving general education and special education students and their families in various capacities of teaching and leadership for grades PK-12.

Maisha graduated from Eastern Kentucky University with a Bachelor's Degree in Early Childhood: Interdisciplinary and a Minor in Special Education. While attending Central Michigan University, Maisha received her Masters Degree in the area of Instruction in Education and her Specialist Degree in Educational Leadership, as well as having her Teacher Leader Endorsement from the State of Georgia.

Maisha and her husband, Winston, have 3 beautiful children, (Kemiah, Kayla, and Winston Jr.) and currently live in the metro Atlanta area.